CUTTING THE STEMS

BY VIRGINIE LALUCQ

TRANSLATED FROM THE FRENCH BY
CLAIRE MCQUERRY AND CÉLINE BOURHIS

(Sb) saturnalia | BOOKS

Distributed by Independent Publishers Group
Chicago

Saturnalia Books
105 Woodside Rd.
Ardmore, PA 19003
info@saturnaliabooks.com

ISBN: 978-1-947817-58-6 (print), 978-1-947817-59-3 (ebook)
Library of Congress Control Number: 2023933345

Cover art and book design by Robin Vuchnich

Distributed by:
Independent Publishing Group
814 N. Franklin St.
Chicago, IL 60610
800-888-4741

ACKNOWLEDGEMENTS

The translators are grateful to the following journals, in which excerpts of this translation have appeared:

"January/Janvier/Januar/Enero" sec. 4-14, *Denver Quarterly Review.*
"December/Décembre/Deciembre/Dezember," *Double Change.*

We are grateful also to Virginie Lalucq, who supported the work throughout this long process, and who was more than willing to offer feedback and guidance. Many thanks to the poet and translator Cynthia Hogue for her encouragement and support of the project over the years.

Translators' Introduction

I first corresponded with Virginie Lalucq in 2006, when we were both young poets and I was just beginning some forays into translation. Lalucq had already published two books of some notice in France, including *Fortino Sámano*, a collaboration with the renowned French philosopher Jean-Luc Nancy. Perhaps it speaks to the level of my enthusiasm, but when I wrote to inquire about an English translation, Lalucq was willing to trust her poetry to an American student with little experience. In those early stages of our communication, she cautioned me that *Couper les Tiges* (*Cutting the Stems*), her first book, was not the easiest work to translate, but I didn't then anticipate *how* challenging the project would be or that, in the end, it would take 16 years to complete.

Lalucq is an experimental poet whose work is eclectic and genre bending, reflected even in performances of her poetry, for which she often collaborates with musicians and sound artists—and her second book, of course, was written in collaboration with a philosopher. Her poetry is frequently metatextual, and it tends to include an element of collage. *Cutting the Stems* is a playful, long poem in sections that contains a pastiche of various unlikely influences: manuals on gardening and plant propagation, etymological dictionaries, gemstone and mineral guides, a how-to for florists, and other "un-poetic" texts. Her style is inventive and elaborate; it defies minimalist poetry while at the same time incorporating some of its characteristics. For instance, she experiments with white space and the isolation of certain words or phrases on the page. She also "prunes" her own text and playfully reminds the reader in footnotes that "It is necessary to attempt more pruning." Lalucq's poetry invites a questioning of poetic convention, foregrounding language's gaps and slippages.

The poem includes the central personas *she* and *he* who at times talk past each other in lyrical and often surrealist exchanges. Through these personas we see gender category as fluid. *She,* whose identity merges with the poem's speaker, is a florist and devotes much attention to the tending of words, to "[her] sentence," which takes on a life of its own. In fact, the French article allows the sentence to be both *she* and *it.* (Though, having to choose in English, we've settled on *it.*) For the speaker/poet cutting the stems of plants is akin to cutting away at language (so that "the sentences bloom").

In *Cutting the Stems,* language's instability is reflected in Lalucq's frequent play with homophony and homonymy and her deconstruction of etymology and idiom. This essential quality of the work is what also makes it so resistant to translation. At times, the work of translating the wordplay seemed impossible. The progress came in starts and stops, and there are many instances where the cleverness and playfulness of the French could not be fully captured.

In the book's second section, for instance, Lalucq has written "Elle n'écrit pas: elle (s') eschine," which we've translated as "She doesn't write: she exhausts (herself)." Here, Lalucq plays on "s'échiner," an idiom with the French word for "spine" comparable to the English expression "to break one's back." It can also mean "to exhaust oneself." Moreover, in changing "échiner" to the homophonic neologism "eschiner," Lalucq echoes her use of "esche" (bait) from earlier in the poem. As she explained in a recent email, the poem's "she" works hard, while also making herself the bait ("so that the words will bite her hook"). In adding parentheses around the reflexive part of the verb, Lalucq suggests an exhaustion of self as well as a non-reflexive exhaustion, in this case, of language—a reference to French filmmaker and essayist Georges Perec's 1974 *An Attempt at Exhausting a Place in Paris,* a record of Perec's observations while sitting for many hours in Saint Sulpice Square. Finally, "s'eschiner" is also sonically close to the Old French word *"Meschine"* (mistress) of the poem's subsequent line. While our translation retains an essential part of Lalucq's original intent, it sacrifices much of the play with sound and the more densely layered meanings just outlined. Though we considered several other solutions, we decided that the exhaustion of self/language was the most important element to preserve.

There were many passages like this one in which we had to sacrifice some of Lalucq's original music or cleverness. To make the task more challenging, Lalucq's text has a web-like quality to it, the wordplay in one passage often relying on earlier images and instances of word play, so that to tug on a single thread of the translation often meant unraveling other threads. Consider, for instance, our struggle with "seichement" (p.9 of reverse) and "s aiche ment," (p.19), both homophonic portmanteaus, combining "sèchement" (dryly) with "seiche" (cuttlefish) and with "aiche" (bait), respectively. To write something "sèchement" is to write it concisely, in a brusque tone. However, a literal translation of Lalucq's word would be "she writes cuttelfishedly," a nonsense phrase in English. In French, the statement is playful in a more meaningful way, a comment about writing style that echoes the text's other references to fish and bones. The second, related play-on-words with "aiche," again *sounds like* "sèchement" but takes up the motif of bait (for which "esche" and "aiche" are alternate spellings).

The challenge, then, was to devise a somewhat equally meaningful form of wordplay in English. It was a challenge that seemed insurmountable. I would make lists of English adverbs containing homophones for "bait," none of which came close to a satisfying fit. It was this particular problem spot, along with a few others, that led me many times over the years to close the book and walk away from the work, deciding that, while certain isolated passages could be translated, the whole complicated web simply couldn't be remade in another language.

After a several-year gap in our correspondence, Lalucq reached out again in early 2022 with an eagerness to finish the work, and I had, at that time, the good fortune to find a collaborator in colleague and native speaker Céline Bourhis. Bourhis's insights into cultural references and certain nuances of the language made the work once again seem possible. Thanks to a discussion of the contexts for "sèchement," for instance, we found a satisfying answer in "acerbically," which, while offering no easy wordplay with bones or species of fish, did allow the sonic slip from "bic" to "beak." With a revision to my translation of "*leur clouer le bec*" (p.8), from the colloquial "shutting them up" back to the more literal "shutting their beaks," we created the set-up for the beak/bic slip when it occurred. As for the second hurdle, while "acerbically" has no homophonic ties to "bait," "acerbate," which derives from the same Latin root, does, expanding the poem's linguistic web enough to approximate the original.

It is hard to believe that this project of so many years has finally drawn to a close. The work has been a pleasure and a task that frequently demonstrates, as Lalucq writes, that "words are there as reminders that they escape us, as soon as we believe they've bitten the hook."

—Claire McQuerry and Céline Bourhis

Table of Contents

One day, unbeknownst to her superiors, she succeeded at her life's greatest experiment: creating a putrescible, breakable, stainable thread.

— I —

DECEMBER / DÉCEMBRE / DICIEMBRE / DEZEMBER

1998

1

(She writes)
She doesn't write: she renudes

she hides her breasts after
during
before

2

She doesn't write:
She is beautiful like a pinch at the heart

she dries the text from afar
Rita Hayworth, you know!

3

I Do The Washing Up
my text's come undone

I dry the text from afar

I didn't have time to do the cuffs!
(So my sentence spoke

4

my sentence, the world's most ephemeral,
it's restless,
it has the wanderlust,
my gyspum-sentence

slips away quietly

5

She says HER   though she could very well say HIM

There are as many i's in HER as in

              HIM

6

              She always ejaculates prematurely

but rarely

She says scary things because things are scary

7

For instance, she says: "Do you want to arm wrestle me?"

                    She doesn't like releasing her own sperm.

                    Or that of others, either.

8

She says this as well:

                    "a bladder, that's not sexy!"

And this:

                    "I dance with orthopedic soles"

          She doesn't put a condom on her words: they go limp from the first

9

He always says "it's good, you know…."
    as if she understood…what?

He always says "you question it!"
    as if she understood…what?

                that the answers exist?

10

He tells her, you know, all day long I wondered how you might be dressed
today…
and this, also: my powder, it's ivory in shade

11

She would have said: I *love you* like a rear-view mirror

                              a discarded bra

on the bed
She would have said: I *love you* like a bottleneck
oh my phrase lathe

                    but, tonight, she had no words:
                    on the date, nothing but *Curtains*

12

my phrase frays   she doesn't know the song

except *Tiny Tears*, and *She's Gone,* of course, *She's gone*

(*and it's quiet now*[1]

13

                                    Wie einst Lili Marlene

                                 Wie einst Lili Marlene[2]

14

                She knows just one sentence:

15

                             She never says: *I love you*

                     She says: it's because of your skin

16

                     She's a florist, florist by profession

                  The part of her work she loves best?

           Cutting the stems. and shutting *their* beaks

              (shutting *their* beaks of the words

17

        my sentence,

18

my sentence doesn't believe in the existence of a possible glass but rather
in things that shatter and the ones that break you. also. bones.

19

        She writes acerbeakally

20

        She cries out in fear

for example, she doesn't say: criminetly!

        but yick-yick, yeyey

        or even crudacrudacrud

21

Every two or three months   —it's rather cruel, I confess—
he organizes murders in his living room, but it's for a good cause:

                    he does it to overcome his phobia of blood
                    you have many more (sentences) like this?

22

She's all thumbs

                        it's an inconvenience:
               she often has blood left on her hands
               and the blotters do nothing to help.
             When I told you that she was scary!

23[1]

Murder   consists of an echo
precise handwriting   take the pulse of
the words   cut
their carotid   and you will have my formula for blood:

23²

Blood formula: $Fe_3A_2Si_3O_{12}$. extreme mental fortitude. severely pronounced mythomania. Innate sense of arithmetic: spends his time inventing tall tales

23³

countdown

likes dotting the i's

(and the records

23⁴

It's the garnet part of her that offends

Satisfied yet?

24

The day he received a life certificate from the city hall he realized it was
a good time for him

to set the record straight

25

He had his doll Bella in his arms

oblique and menacing
as a glance

26

She hadn't said "I love you" but "not like you think,"

the *giregrine*!

27

The day he saw it was impossible for someone to love him   he
grabbed his doll Bella and smothered her with kisses   tore off
her arms   Then he took his pen, tried not to cry and continued on

There were too many a's
There were too many i's

28

The day his father suggested that he throw away his childhood drawings, I
understood that this was growing up: to amputate a leg

29

It was just a suggestion, really. A way to free up space. But it's wonderful
to have one's two legs. it's wonderful* to have legs. in any case

---

* *Remove wonderful*

think s he could walk now

think s he could walk

30

the word she hates the most in your language?

: **neutrality**

and **disintegrate.** which is nearly the same thing. the words she prefers?

: **cover**

in cover, there is **bare**

there is **arrayed**

and a missile

rhododendron

31

a tree   **rhodo**

a rose   **dendron**

a carnation a poem

incarnation of poem

an organdy orgasm

in the metro

— II —

JANUARY / JANVIER / ENERO / JANUAR

1999

1

An angiosperm's lifecycle
he would have said

2

you are lovely

you are lovely like a *pinchmaker*

you are lovely like rosemary you are lovely like the bird with a brittle
heart you are lovely like the rock the pond the carp

you are lovely like the bait dangled
on a hook

3

He would have said: you write that how, "a cer bait?"

4

She doesn't write:
she renudes

she's *carp* a cious

5

There's a position of language:
There's a position of the skin

6

She doesn't write:

she exhausts (herself)

7

She writes:

Meschine Mitleid miskîn[3]

8

She doesn't write she says:

— excuse me if my hands are wet, but this morning I have a date with a multifunctional sentence

— a sentence light as gypsophila

sea mist, you know!

9

She doesn't wear mascara:
black is her natural color

10

I repeat she's a florist,
florist by profession

                                    and sea falcon,
                                        accessorily

11

I still recall the sight of her leaving her bathroom

                                    the sea mist

12

With a knapsack on her back   one might call her a little girl

13

Gymnotus or gypsophila,
what difference?

                                maybe in the stiletto h eel ?

14[1]

She was hitchhiking, the sea mist, when I saw her on the side of the road. The light was long as a red skirt. So I gave her a ride, the little girl with menacing eyes

> *what's with that menacing look?*
> *Giregrine, shoo!*

14[2]

> When she powders her face, the sea mist, it's so quiet!

15[1]

convertible open   (Zippo ah)
Zippo ah   variable geometry

O my hitchhiker

opening yourself on this emergency turnout:
what could I have done but unlatch my hood?
infinitely, infinitely

15[2]

O my hitchhiker!

> you don't write
> you nude
> on your Minitel rouge[4]

16

You speak correctly
You listen well
but do you know how to only look?

17

Writing consists of listening
of listening very closely to things
Listening's not the same thing as auscultating. but

asyndeta gentle asyndeta

asyndeta

I will pluck your feathers![5]

18

When he asked, "how do you dress in the summer?" she didn't dare say, "naked; totally naked; with my nakedness. and sometimes with a swimsuit in place of pasties."

So she said: "with colors."
"red and basswood green."

What a prim-rose
this girl!

19

He could have retorted:
I love this gesture, when you unfasten your sentence like this....
Here's what he did

Oh my little wolf! Oh my lupanar!

20

If she hadn't been a florist,
she would have been a rose garden   a wild rose garden

or a dancer

go-go dancer in a field ( ) poppies

21

But she relied too much on sight, on what her sentence resembled, while she
unfastened it, all alone, in front of her mirror

22

She would have said:

Hands in the air! Rabbit hair!

The mistress in her swimming wear![6]

And he would have raised his arms

23

He would have said you're lovely,   you're lovely like a terminal a punch

clock of explosions   oh my giregrine,

all dressed in organdy!

24

So I took—**alouette, gentle, alouette!**[7]—my wings to my neck and I fled!

25

If only I'd declared my flight
on the stairs

26

I was nothing but a vol-au-vent
a rosebay
the bait abandoned
on the bank of a pond

27

Declaring his love   was an affront?

28

what she wears in the summer?
dresses, lyrical dresses
and low-cut words
light like gypsophila

29

                                                            and when it rains?

a simple clematis
in her hair

30

                    a clematis hairlines her temples

: she doesn't write

: she nudes

the skirt split in back

to write is an affair for horticulturists
or hydrangeas

Writing is a gardenia-party

Precisions
(When I refine my etymologies)

0   It's *horticulturess* that can't be said

1   This isn't an anthology, but a collection of action-flowers

2   The action-flower? An action-sentence akin to gypsophila:
        a sentence, that is to say: with similarities to gypsum

3   A sentence, then,
        and one under a permanent threat

4   that of becoming chalky

5   a sentence of calcareous origin
        fragile friable

6   prunable*, one hopes

7   a gypsosentence

---

* *It is necessary to attempt more pruning*

 # 8   The gypsophilic action?
An action flooded with love,
as much as it could be a punch clock

 # 9   an action that's dehydrated
dehydrating
particularly soluble in water

10   Furthermore (on the one hand)

11   Gypsum is the mineral-equivalent of organdy

12   Organdy is the fabric-equivalent of gypsum

13   Gypsophila is the floral-equivalent of organdy

14   This implies that

15   as gypsum is a variety of organdy

16   so gypsophila is a variety of organdy.

17   Therefore, gypsophila is a variety of gypsum.

 # 18   Furthermore (on the other hand)

 # 19   In the word *organdy*, there is the word *gardon*. and a shared
            obscurity

 # 20   It follows that these two specimens knew how to evade the
            expert fishing poles of our most astute lexicologists

 # 21   Voila! Here, I open my Picoche[8] for you

 # 22   GARDON 13th c.: *Obsolete* < French *gardon*, uncertain origin:
            perhaps Germanic: a commonality with the verb *guard* (this fish
            guards against that which frightens it) is conjectural.

 # 23   ORGANDY 18th c.: < French, origin unknown.

 # 24[1] But any dative ethic there is,
            will be of no help to me

 # 24[2] **Because** words are there as reminders that they escape us,
            as soon as we believe they've bitten the hook!*

---

* *(It is necessary to attempt more pruning)*

 # 25 There's no need:
—if it's about a cotton cloth, fine and very filmy, finished
with a stiff sizing, add

That, everyone knows

 # 26 As hypothesis, 1723 poss. alter. of var. of var. of *organza*, I
specify: imposs. this question

 # 27 Here cotton cloth

 # 28 In neither case silk thread

 # 29 *Cyprinid*, if need be,

 # 30 *able*

That organdy could be the same fabric in silk, yes, I know, and
that this might explain the fact of *alter. of var. of var. of organza*, I
know but deny it yes

 # 31 *pruned prun'*

32   That *organzine* was a twisted silk thread, designed for forming
        silk yarn, no one ignores, but this resolves nothing

33   no equally appealing hypothesis exists
        So, I disagree with

34   Diachronically synchronically

35   I prefer the cotton mystery

36   Moreover, no one would dream of
        tying organdy's origin to *cottone*
        on the basis of cotton thread
        whereas
        (It is necessary to attempt more pruning)

37   **No one**
        what, then, to make of the list *cotton fabrics*
        (broadcloth, cambric, calico, crepe, cretonne, damask, fustian,
        gabardine, gauze, gingham, linen, lawn, madras, percale, poplin,
        piqué, pointelle, sateen, shirting, tarlatan, terry, twill, voile,
        zephyr)?

 # 38   How can I help that I love freshwater fabrics, with 1220 lining
and a cloudy transparency
: muslin

 # 39   In contrast, heated to 950°, gypsum yields plaster of Paris,
which absorbs water but will harden in 24 hours

 # 40   The flower is in a bouquet of great lightness

 # 41   Furthermore (On the other hand)
Given that this text is about precision and that to precisionize
is to cut (the stems) again: one will cut the sentence in two, in
saying that words also have stems and that their great pleasure
is to be cut. very often.

 # 42   And the sentences in all of this?

 # 43   During this time the sentences bloom

 # 44   their beaks in the air

 # 45   lilacs*

---

* *It is necessary to attempt more pruning*

46   A rosery of Vs consists of a vibrant punctuation
could there be a rosery of Vs in a flight of cranes?
maybe,
without doubt,
I won't say!

47   I'll content myself with issuing counterfeit bills

48   *a web of lies,* to write is always, is always to bank up more lies.
completely

49   "cluster all these individuals together"

50   and the commas, imagine that!

51   dancing the cha-cha
snowflakes
in the already blossoming
plum trees

52   in openlucht fermentation
in the open air I'd say in the open air
swarm

53   lilacs cluster
        buzz
        perfume

54   fermentation and mauve very very
        cloth hurling
        of

55   This nausea
        of the finish line
        lilac

56   lilac fermentation
        color
        I announce the

57   but slice*
        in the marrow
        of the subject

---

* *It is necessary to attempt more pruning*

 # 58¹   tibia

I diagnose you

in the stiffness of the muscle

ankylosic

 # 58²   I stretch

I warm up   my articulations

 # 59   see it's this bony

tissue

that withstands the smell

 # 60   one must cut it

 # 61   heady lilacs buzzing has nothing to do with lily + honeysuckle

+ a hint of garnet has nothing to do with blackcurrant

blueberry slate and mauve and gin neither juniper berries

nor you

not capsule not lilac

62   uproot it, then chew
        writing is that decay
        and which ferments, odor

63   cadaver cluster wisteria
        an odor like

64   Fermentatiebak
        would be this

65   a fermentation vat,
        writing

66   lilac

**Now, I need, a text that's scalloped in its century:**

 # 67   There are thoughts like that, thoughts as grave
            as violets
            thoughts of stretched   velvet
            There are thoughts like that so very violet so very stretched
            that they blacken from it   struck
            There are thoughts like that and others as light* as gypsophila
            they annihilate yellow and orange

And then not   **After all,**

 # 68   clematises

 # 69   clematises are Ranunculaceae

---

[*] *It is necessary to attempt more pruning*

70   little frogs
        rescinded have which
        the flower bed of thoughts

71   pensive pansies

72   thoughts are violet

73   voila! I open my dicotyledons for you

74   Of their sub-phylum spermatophyte

                                            the one is dialypetalous
                                    and the other settles for five

75   their ovules are enclosed & the seeds locked in their fruits
        You don't believe me?
        All of this is searchable
        I have my conscience with me   in my Webster's Abridged

76   of elongated ungues and petals five
         the caryophyllaceae

77   the caryophyllaceae

78   gypsophila is Caryophyllaceae

79   The process consists of heating it to 120°, after which it loses
         ¾ of its water. The resulting powder, put in contact with water,
         reabsorbs what it has lost and before solidifying, forms a plastic
         mass used in all casting processes. Heated to 200°, gypsum loses
         all of its water as well as the faculty to reabsorb it.
         This new form is called anhydrite, variety that occurs in nature.

80   so much so that its airy blooms have given it the name "baby's
         breath."
         The inflorescences of all gypsophila are used for softening the
         floral compositions with which they are associated. Those of
         gypsophila paniculata dry without difficulty for winter bouquets.

81   one can also equip oneself with a gypsometer
to measure the gypsum content of sentences

82 $CaSO_4 \, 2H_2O$ is the formula for the herbaceous plant that has
for its name

83   a bony configuration

84   calcium sulfate

85   *phila*
of white flowers

86   *gyspum*

87   the white suit woman with :

88   The most well-known use of gypsum is the fabrication of plaster
for casting. Called "Mary's glass" in Catholic countries of the
Mediterranean, one hangs fragments of it on statues of the Virgin
to symbolize purity.

89   Pardon me but in hindsight
        I prefer *gyspum*
        to gypsum:
        it's prettier and moreover conforms
        to my dyslexia

90   Mine
        the woman with*

91   Mine
        By the Sign in

92   rose harsh rose

93   apetalous rose my

94   Natural anhydrite is thus anhydrous calcium sulfate, that is,
        without water. Crystalized in the orthorhombic system, it has
        three cleavages at right angles.

---

* *It is necessary to attempt more pruning*

95   dyslexically

96   again

97   *giregrine*

98   and change nothing in the definition

99   then I am a female Peregrine

100   *Geregrine, shoo!*

101   yeah and "I feel like a night bird that refuses to roost even after circling three flights,"* besides!

102   besides, The owl whistles: it's an enthusiast of whistles

besides, My text whistles, it's an enthusiast of whistles

---

* Li Qingzhao, *Flowers of the Cinnamon Tree,* trans. to French from the Chinese by Zheng Su, Orphée, 1990

103   I osprey you osprey s/he ospreys we osprey

104   Mine by
the right
of

105   your rhodosentence   **by the right**
leaves some bruises   **of the White Election!**

106   and no choice

107   because without stems

108   : a minimum stripped bare*

---

* *It is necessary to attempt more pruning*

109   — Oh stop sacrificing yourself!

— But no, I'm sorry, I'm not wasting away!

110   **Shh**! It's me who's whispering !

111   Nyctalope![9]

112   Yes!

113   Nyctalope!

114   Yes!

115   Shoot, I have my tulips!

116   I don't like it when you've got your tulips!

117   Shh, it's me who's whispering!

118   Nyctalope!

119   Yes!

120   Nyctalope!

121   Yes!

122   The whisperer is me

123   The whisperer

 # 124   If I write the rhododendron is a tree of roses.
The rose laurel is a rosy tree.
Rosemary is a variety of mist. (marine).
Marine mist is a variety of gypsophila.

 # 125   Indeed, you'll have understood that this project has more to do
with rhodoid

 # 126   To ensure that I am justified in saying:

 # 127   There is no gypsophilic action
WITHOUT rhodofying* action

 # 128   There isn't gypsum except with rose
There isn't a thing but rhodophrasing

 # 129   in all florideae

 # 130   Florideae is a variety of marine rose.
In other words, a thorny subject!
and extremely calcareous!

---

* (rhodifying = roseifying): this is rhodiumizing

| # 131 | half-seaweed | half-rhodo |
| | half-rose | half-phyta |

| # 132 | based on acetate of rhodia* |
| | a celluloid experiment |

| # 133 | transparent and combustible | hybrid |

---

* It is necessary to attempt more pruning

134   I work, you work, we work in the rose industry,
        o my rosegrower!

135   workers among the workers
        in the rosegarden-hive

136   We fabricate petal-mechanisms
        of sepal-horology

137   and we own nothing

138   if it's nothing but the words that own us

139   Oh my rosegrower! IOU
        as a rosebay in a rosebed
        rose rose rose from the dead
        this rosebud-lay
        rose to the bait
        just for you

140   To avoid decay—what a crazy idea—remove any leaves at the
base of the stem.*

141   : this is the propagation of cuttings:

142   Eliminate the leaves from the bottom 2/3 of the stem.

143   Limit the length of the cutting to between 7 and 15 cm, depending
on the species, trimming directly beneath a leaf.

144   Always remove a growth from the end, if possible one that has
not flowered.

145   : this is the propagation of cuttings:

146   to take root and become a separate plant.

147   Of course, one could also layer

148   But that is a much more intimate** affair

---

* It is necessary to attempt more pruning

** intimidating, incalculable

 # 149   an affair of layering

 # 150   consists of causing roots to grow from a branch without detaching it from the parent plant.

In this way it stays nourished by the plant until it is capable of supplying its own nutrients.

It is only at this moment that it is "severed," that is, detached.

 # 151   : this is layering :

 # 152   a process that strongly resembles the propagation of cuttings but includes many fewer risks.

153   Of course, there are different kinds of layering

—mound layering (especially recommended for many ornamental shrubs and for fruit rootstock development)*

—air layering (often advised for Ficus, **philodendrons**, aralias, etc. whose bases are bare of leaves, but equally applicable to all ornamental shrubs and trees, conifers, etc.)**

154   But personally, I prefer
trench layering

155   Applicable to all species
with branches supple enough to bend,
trench layering consists of

---

* Quinces, apple trees, plum trees… Take the parent plant down: *i.e.* by **cutting (couper)** to 10/15 cm from the ground (in winter): this causes new branches to appear from the dormant buds. In May, as soon as you have a growth of a dozen cm, mound the cluster with dirt or better yet, with a half-and-half mix of sand and peat.

** After having, if necessary, eliminated any encumbering leaves, surround **the stem (la tige)** with a polyethylene film, maintained at top and bottom by a ligature, and fill it with a fairly moist, half-and-half mixture of sand and peat.

 # 156 Burying a low offshoot in a small trench dug near the plant's base and kept in place with a hook driven into hard soil.

 # 157 Uncover and lift its end out vertically and secure it to a stake. Eliminate the leaves from the buried portion. Refill the trench with a half-and-half mixture of sand and peat.

: This is trench layering :

Incision*

↙

_____

* *To prune: the action of pruning*

0 It's pacemaker that can't be said

Final clippings

Several cardiac pacemakers have regulated my workings along this ramble, namely:

1   gypsophila

2   The reading of *Guide Clause (Practical gardening treatise,* Serge Vadé, edited by L. Clause, 21ˢᵗ edition, 1976) to which precisions **# 80, # 148 - # 158** owe much, aided by *Minerals and Rocks* (Karen Callisen, French adaptation by Jean Orcel and André Ph. Sandrea, Fernand Nathan, collection "New Guides for the Naturalist," 1976) cf. precisions **# 39, # 79, # 88, # 95,** and finally an article found in a *Télé 7 Jours* (TV Guide) dated from April 2000 (*Multiply Your Plants,* by Patrick Mioulane), which was largely the inspiration for precisions **# 141 - # 147.** Furthermore, precisions **# 22** and **# 23** owe their existence to the *French Etymological Dictionary* (Jacqueline Picoche, Robert, 1986); precisions **# 25 - # 32** and **# 37** are indebted to *Petit Robert* (1988 edition).

3   ROSE TREE very distinctly tagged in neon pink
            on a green fir (evergreen trunks x 2)
            on the route of *Gros de ça* et de *Pompoms* (Morvan)

4   The bouquet of lilacs (mauve and + a fragrance matching garnet)
            which, on bus 61, between Austerlitz and Ledru-Rollin (direction Port des Lilas),*

5   **The author gives thankful acknowledgment to these.**

---

* *Quid sit lilac lumen?* From where does the lilac()light come? Is it in the decay or the color? (an odor close to). One responds, for the present, that the lilac is in no way a lily. only an Oleaceae.

To avoid decay
remove the leaves at the base
of the stem.

Translators' Endnotes on Text

1 These and *Curtains* above are references to songs by Tindersticks

2 Reference to the Marlene Dietrich song "Lili Marleen."

3 Meschine: from Old French, "young girl" or "mistress, concubine"--derived from Arabic "mîskin" (poor).

4 The Minitel box was France's precursor to the Internet. The "Minitel Rose" was a popular Minitel service offering adult chat lines.

5 Altered lyrics from the French children's song "Alouette"

6 A common children's playground rhyme in France

7 We have chosen to preserve the "alouette" (French for "lark") here as it appears in the original text, as the French song is somewhat known by English speakers, and the wordplay of asyndeta / alouette is untranslatable.

8 French etymological dictionary

9 Though "nyctalope" is an obsolete word in English, its French cognate is still used to describe a class of animals with the ability to see better at night.

Virginie Lalucq was born in 1975 and lives in Paris. She is the author of *Couper les tiges* (Act Mem/ Comp'act, 2001) and *Fortino Sámano, Les débordements du poème* (with Jean-Luc-Nancy, Galilée 2004) translated by Sylvain Gallais and Cynthia Hogue (Omnidawn, 2012). She has been a member of the editorial collective for the journal *Nioques* for twenty years.

Claire McQuerry's poetry and translations have appeared in *Denver Quarterly Review, Tin House, Gettysburg Review, Poetry Northwest, Permafrost,* and other journals. Her poetry collection *Lacemakers* (Southern Illinois University Press) won the Crab Orchard First Book Prize and was a finalist for the Washington State Book Award. She has been the recipient of fellowships from the Virginia Center for the Creative Arts, the Sewanee Writers' Workshop, the Dorothy Sargent Rosenberg Prizes, and the Virgnia G. Piper Center for Creative Writing. She is an Assistant Professor at Bradley University.

Céline Bourhis is a lecturer at Bradley University where she teaches global literature and technical writing courses. Her research interests include postcolonial studies, postmodern literature, and life writing. Prior to her teaching appointment, she worked as an editorial assistant at Dalkey Archive Press and published interviews with authors in Context.

Also by Claire McQuerry

Lacemakers (Southern Illinois University Press 2012).

Also by Virginie Lalucq

Fortino Sámano, Les débordements du poème (with Jean-Luc-Nancy, Galilée 2001)

Fortino Sámano: The overflowing of the Poem, (with Jean-Luc Nancy, translated by Sylvain Gallais and Cynthia Hogue, Omnidawn 2004)

Cutting The Stems is printed in Adobe Garamond Pro.
www.saturnaliabooks.org

Préface à moi-même : couper court (toujours).

—

Pour Claire et Céline,
mes courageuses traductrices !

TABLE

Un jour, à l'insu de sa direction, elle
réussit l'expérience de sa vie : créer
une fibre textile cassable, salissable
et putrescible

— I —

December / Décembre / Diciembre / Dezember

1998

1

(Elle écrit)

Elle n'écrit pas : elle renude

elle se cache les seins après

avant

pendant

2

Elle n'écrit pas :

Elle est belle comme un pincement au cœur

elle sèche le texte au large

Rita Hayworth, quoi !

3

I Do The Washing Up

mon texte est décousu

je sèche le texte au large

j'ai pas eu le temps d'en faire les revers !

(*Ainsi parlait ma phrase*

4

ma phrase, la plus éphémère au monde,

elle ne tient pas en place,

elle a la bougeotte,

ma phrase-gyspe

se file en douce

5

Elle dit ELLE   mais elle pourrait très bien dire IL
Il y a autant de i dans ELLE que dans
                    IL

6

                    Elle éjacule toujours précocement
mais pas souvent.

Elle dit des choses effrayantes parce que les choses sont effrayantes

7

Par exemple, elle dit : « tu veux faire un bras de fer avec moi ? »
                              Elle n'aime pas lécher son propre sperme.
                                        Et celui des autres, non plus.

8

Elle dit encore ceci :
                              « une vessie, ça n'est pas sexy ! »
Et ceci :
                              « je danse avec des semelles orthopédiques »

        Elle ne met pas de préservatif sur ses mots : ils débandent aussitôt

9

Il dit toujours « c'est bon, tu sais…. »

comme si elle savait … quoi ?

Il dit toujours « tu en poses des questions ! »

comme si elle savait … quoi ?

que les réponses existent ?

10

Il lui dit tu sais, je me suis demandé toute la journée comment tu pouvais
bien être habillée aujourd'hui…

et ceci, encore : ma poudre, c'est ivoire, le coloris.

11

Elle aurait dit : je *taime* comme un rétroviseur

un soutien-gorge

sur le tapis

Elle aurait dit :   je *taime* comme un goulot d'étranglement

o mon tourneur-fraiseur

mais, ce soir-là, les mots lui manquaient :

il n'y avait que *curtains* au rendez-vous

12

ma phrase-fraise   elle ne connaît pas la chanson

mais *Tiny Tears* seulement, et *She's gone*, bien sûr, *She's gone*

(and it's quiet now

13

Wie einst Lili Marlene

Wie einst Lili Marlene

14

Elle ne connait qu'une phrase :

15

Elle ne dit jamais : *je t'aime*

Elle dit : c'est à cause de ta peau

16

Elle est fleuriste, fleuriste de profession.

Ce qu'elle préfère dans son métier ?

couper les tiges. et *leur* clouer le bec.

(clouer *leur* bec aux mots

17

ma phrase,

18

ma phrase, elle ne croit pas en l'existence d'un verre possible mais
plutôt aux choses qui se brisent et à celles qui vous brisent. aussi.
les os.

19

Elle écrit seichement.

20

Elle pousse des cris d'effroi

par exemple, elle ne dit pas : Scrongneugnieu !

mais yick-yick, yéhyé,

ou encore kéckékéck

21

Tous les deux-trois mois   —c'est assez cruel, j'en conviens—

il organise des meurtres dans son salon, mais c'est pour la bonne cause :

il fait ça pour vaincre sa phobie du sang

t'en as encore beaucoup des (phrases) comme ça ?

22

Elle est assez gauchère   c'est un inconvénient :

elle a souvent du sang qui lui reste sur les mains

et les buvards n'y font rien.

Quand je vois disais qu'elle était effrayante !

23[1]

Le meurtre   consiste en une écho

graphie précise   tâtez le pouls des

mots   tranchez-en

la carotide   et vous obtiendrez ma formule sanguine :

23²

Formule sanguine : $Fe_3Al_2Si_3O_{12}$. très fort mental. mythomanie sévèrement prononcée. Sens de l'arithmétique inné : passe son temps à inventer des contes à dormir debout.

23³

compte à rebours

aime mettre les points sur les i

(et les pendules

23⁴

C'est son côté escarboucle qui rebiffe

Alors, *satisfait ?*

24

Le jour où il reçut un certificat de vie de sa mairie, il comprit qu'il était grand temps pour lui

de mettre les pendules à l'heure

25

Il avait sa poupée Bella dans les bras

oblique et menaçante

comme un regard

26

Elle n'avait pas dit « je vous aime » mais « pas comme tu penses »,

La *girargue* !

27

Le jour où il comprit qu'il était impossible qu'on l'aimât   il se
saisit de sa poupée Bella la couvrit de baisers   lui arracha les
bras   Puis il prit son stylo s'efforça de ne pas pleurer et continua
sur sa lancée

Il y avait trop de *a*

Il y avait trop de *i*

28

Le jour où son père lui suggéra de jeter ses dessins d'enfant, j'ai compris que
c'était ça, grandir : s'amputer d'une jambe.

29

Ça n'était qu'une suggestion, en effet, une suggestion pour faire de la place.
Mais c'est merveilleux d'avoir ses deux jambes. c'est merveilleux* d'avoir des
jambes. de toute façon.

---

* *Ôtez merveilleux.*

think s he could walk now

think s he could walk

30

le mot qu'elle déteste le plus dans votre langue ?

: **neutralité**

et **désintégrer**. ce qui est à peu près la même chose. les mots qu'elle
préfère ?

: **couvrir**

dans couvrir, il y a **dénudé**

Il y a **revêtu**

et un missile format

rhododendron

31

un arbre   **rhodo**

une rose   **dendron**

un œillet un poème

un œil let le poème

un orgasme d'organdi

dans le métro

– II –

JANUARY / JANVIER / ENERO / JANUAR

1999

1

Le temps d'une angiosperme
il aurait dit

2

tu es belle

tu es belle comme un *pincemaker*

tu es belle comme le romarin tu es belle come un oiseau fragile
du cœur tu es belle comme la roche l'étang le gardon

tu es belle come l'esche que l'on tend
à l'hameçon

3

il aurait dit : tu écris ça comment, « s aiche ment » ?

4

Elle n'écrit pas :
elle renude

c'est une b *esche* use

5

Il y a une position du langage :

Il y a une position de la peau

6

Elle n'écrit pas :

elle (s') eschine

7

Elle écrit :

Meschine Mitleid miskin

8

Elle n'écrit pas elle dit :

— excusez-moi si j'ai les mains trempées mais, ce matin, j'ai

normalement rendez-vous avec une phrase-multifonctions

— une phrase légère comme du gypsophile

la rosée marine, quoi !

9

Elle ne porte pas de mascara :

le noir est naturel chez elle

10

Je rappelle qu'elle est fleuriste,
fleuriste de profession

et aigle de mer,

accessoirement

11

Je la revois encore sortir de sa salle de bains

la rosée marine

12

Avec son sac en bandoulière

on aurait dit une petite fille

13

Gymnote ou gypsophile,
quelle différence ?

peut-être dans le talon aiguille ?

14¹

Elle faisait de l'autostop, la rosée marine, quand je l'ai rencontrée au bord de la chaussée. Le feu était long comme une jupe rouge. Alors, je l'ai prise à mon bord, la petite fille au regard torve.

c'est quoi, ce regard torve ? !
Girargue, va !

14²

Quand elle se repoudre, la rosée marine, c'est d'un silence !

15¹

toit ouvrant   (zippo à)

zippo à   géométrie variable

O mon autostoppeuse

toi t'ouvrant sur cette bande d'arrêt d'urgence :

qu'aurais-je bien pu faire que d'ouvrir mon capot ?

infiniment, infiniment

15²

O mon autostoppeuse !   tu n'écris pas

tu nudes

sur ton minitel rouge

16

Tu parles juste

Tu entends bien

mais sais-tu seulement regarder ?

17

Écrire consiste à écouter.

A écouter au plus près des choses.

Écouter ne veut pas dire ausculter. mais

asyndète gentille asyndète
asyndète
je te plumerai !

18

Quand il a demandé : « comment tu t'habilles l'été ? », elle n'a pas osé lui
répondre : « nue ; toute nue avec ma nudité. et quelquefois, avec un maillot de
bain, en guise de cache-sein. »

Alors elle a dit : « avec des couleurs. »
« rouge et vert tilleul. »

Quelle rose-trémière,

cette fille !

19

Il aurait pu rétorquer :
ce geste, j'aime, quand tu dégrafes ta phrase ainsi...
C'est ce qu'il fit.

ô mon loup !   mon lou   panar !

20

Si elle avait pas fait fleuriste,

elle aurait fait roseraie

roseraie sauvage

ou bien danseuse

gogodanceuse dans un champs ( ) coquelicots

21

Mais elle tenait trop à voir, à quoi elle ressemblait, sa phrase, lorsqu'elle la dégrafait, toute seule, devant son miroir.

22

Elle aurait dit :

Haut les mains ! Peau d'lapin !
La maîtresse en maillot d'bain !

Et il aurait levé les bras.

23

Il aurait dit tu es belle,   tu es belle comme un aérogare un horo
dateur à explosions   ô ma girargue,
tout d'organdi vêtue !

24

Alors j'ai pris—**alouette, gentille, alouette !** – mes ailes à mon cou
et j'ai déguerpi !

25

Pour peu que j'aie déclaré mon envol
dans l'escalier

26

Je n'étais rien qu'un vol-au-vent
un laurier-rose
l'èche jetée
au bord de l'étang

27

Déclarer son amour   était une injure ?

28

ce qu'elle porte l'été ?
des robes, des robes lyriques
et des mots échancrés
légers comme du gypsophile

29

                                                          et quand il pleut ?
une simple clématite
dans les cheveux

30

                        une clématite lui lézarde les tempes

: elle n'écrit pas

: elle nude

le dos fendu dans la jupe

écrire est affaire d'horriculteuse
ou d'hortensia

L'écriture est une gardénia-party

Précisions
(Quand je travaille mes étymologies)

 # 0   C'est *horticultrice* qui ne se dit pas

 # 1   Ceci n'est pas une anthologie, mais un recueil d'actions-fleurs.

 # 2   L'action-fleur ? une action-phrase à la mesure du gypsophile :
une phrase, c'est-à-dire : en affinité avec le gypse.

 # 3   Une phrase, donc,
et qui vit sous une menace permanente.

 # 4   celle de devenir plâtreuse.

 # 5   une phrase d'origine calcaire
fragile friable

 # 6   qu'on souhaite égalable *

 # 7   une gypsophrase

---

* *Il faut aller vers plus d'élagation*

 # 8   L'action gypsophile ?

Un action débordante d'amour,

autant que peut l'être un horodateur

 # 9   une action déshydratée

déshydratante

particulièrement soluble dans l'eau

10 Par ailleurs (d'une part)

11 Le gypse est l'équivalent-minéral de l'organdi

12 L'organdi est l'équivalent-tissu du gypse

13 Le gypsophile est l'équivalent-fleur de l'organdi

14 Ceci implique que

15 le gypse est une variété d'organdi

16 Or le gypsophile est une variété d'organdi

17 Donc le gypsophile est une variété de gypse.

 # 18   Par ailleurs (d'une autre part)

 # 19   Dans « organdi » il y a « gardon ». et une obscurité commune.

 # 20   Ce faisant, ces deux spécimens ont su défier la cane à pêche
experte de nos lexicologues les plus pointus

 # 21   Voilà voilà je t'ouvre mon Picoche

 # 22   GARDON, XIIIe s. : mot obscur, p-ê. d'origine germ. : un
rapport avec le verbe *garder* (ce poisson se *garderait* de ce qui
l'effarouche) semble bien conjectural.

 # 23   ORGANDI XVIIIe s. : origine inconnue.

#24[1]   Mais tout datif éthique qui soit,
ne me sera d'aucune aide

#24[2]   **Car** les mots sont là pour nous rappeler qu'ils nous échappent,
sitôt qu'on les croit mordre à l'hameçon ! *

---

* *(Il faut aller vers plus d'elongation)*

#25 Nul n'est besoin :

- qu'il s'agit d'une toile de coton, légère et très claire, enduite d'un apprêt ferme, ajouter

Ça, tout l'monde sait.

 # 26 Pour l'hypothèse 1723 p-ê. altér. d'une var. d'une var. d'*organsin*, je précise : imposs. ici question

#27 Ici toile de coton

 # 28 En aucun cas fil de soie

 # 29 *Cyprinidé*, a la rigueur,

 # 30 able

Que l'organdi pût être le même tissu en soie, oui je le sais, et que cela pût expliquer le fait *altér. d'une var. d'une var. d'organsin*, je le sais mais le nie oui

 # 31 élagu' élagu'

 # 32   Que l'*organsin* fût fil de soie torse, destiné à former la chaîne des étoffes, nul ne l'ignore, mais tout ne résout rien

 # 33   toute hypothèse pour autant séduisante ne l'est pas
So, I disagree with

#34   En diachronie, en synchronie

 # 35   Je préfère le mystère coton

 # 36   D'ailleurs, personne ne viendrait à l'idée :
rattacher organdi rattachable à *cottone*
sous prétexte que toile de coton
alors que
(Il faut aller vers plus d'élagation)

 # 37   **Personne**
Et que faire dès lors de la liste *tissu de coton*
(andrinople, batiste, calicot, cellular, coutil, cretonne, éponge, finette, futaine, linon, lustrine, madapolam, nankin, nansouk, percale, pilou, piqué, plumetis, satinette, shirting, tarlatane, vichy, voile, zéphyr) ?

38   Mais que voulez-vous j'aime les tissus d'eau douce

avec doublure 1220

et transparence obscure :

mousseline

39   Par contre, chauffé à 950°, le gypse donne du plâtre de
maçonnerie, qui absorbe l'eau, mais ne durcit qu'en 24 heures.

40   La fleur est dans l'ensemble d'une grande légèreté

41   Par ailleurs (D'une autre part)
Puisqu'il s'agit de faire des précisions et que, préciser, c'est
encore couper (les tiges) : on coupera la phrase en deux en
disant que les mots ont des tiges, eux aussi, et que leur grand
plaisir est de se les faire couper. très souvent.

42   Et les phrases dans tout ça ?

43   Pendant ce temps les phrases florifèrent

44   le bec à l'air

45   lilas*

` Il faut aller vers plus d'élagation

 # 46   Une roseraie de V consiste en une ponctuation vibrante qu'il y
ait une roseraie de V dans un vol de grues ?

peut-être,

sans doute,

moi je ne prononce pas !

 # 47   je me contente d'émettre de la fausse monnaie

 # 48   *a web of lies,* écrire c'est toujours, c'est toujours débiter des
mensonges. complètement.

 # 49   "cluster all these individuals together"

 # 50   et les virgules voyez-vous ça !

 # 51   dansent le cha-cha-cha
flocons de neige
dans les prunus déjà
fleuris

 # 52   in openlucht fermentation
à l'air libre disais-je à l'air libre
essaim

 # 53   lilas cluster
             bourdonnent
             parfum

 # 54   fermentation et mauve très très
             tissu profération
             de

 # 55   Cet écœurement
             de fin de course
             lilac

#56   lilas fermentation
             couleur
             j'annonce la

 # 57   mais tranche*
             dans l'osseux
             du sujet

˙ *Il faut aller vers plus d'élagation*

#58¹   tibia

je te déclare

dans la raideur du muscle

ankylosée

 # 58²   je m'étire

Je m'échauffe   les articulations

 # 59   voyez c'est ce tissu

osseux

qui supporte l'odeur

 # 60   il vous faut le couper

 # 61   entêtant lilac bourdonnement n'a rien à voir avec muguet +

chèvrefeuille + soupçon de grenat n'a rien à voir avec cassis

myrtille ardoise et parme et gin pas plus que baies genièvre

ou toi

non capsule lilas non

62   arrachez le, puis mâchez
l'écriture est cela pourrissement
et qui fermente, odeur

63   cadavre cluster glycine
une odeur comme

64   Fermentatiebak
serait cela

65   un bac à fermentation,
l'écriture

66   lilac

**Maintenant, il me faut, un texte bien échancré dans son siècle :**

 # 67   Il y a des pensées comme ça, des pensées aussi graves
que violettes
des pensées de velours   tendu
Il y a des pensées comme ça tellement violettes tellement tendues
qu'elle en deviennent noir   frappé
Il y a des pensées comme ça et d'autres aussi légères*
que du gypsophile
elles annihilent le jaune et l'orangé

Et puis non   **Après tout,**

 # 68   les clématites

 # 69   les clématites sont renonculacées

---

* *Il faut aller vers plus d'élagation*

 # 70   petites grenouilles

annulé ont qui

le parterre de pensées

 # 71   les pensées

 # 72   les pensées sont violacées

 # 73   voilà voilà je t'ouvre mes dicotylédones

 # 74   De par leur sous-embranchement spermatophyte

l'un est dialypétale

et l'autre se contente de cinq

 # 75   leurs ovules sont enclos & les graines enfermées

dans leurs fruits

Vous ne me croyez pas ?

Tout cela est pourtant consultable

J'ai ma conscience avec moi   dans le Petit Robert

76   à onglet allongé et pétales cinq

les caryophyllacées

77   les caryophyllacées

78   le gypsophile est caryophyllacée

79   L'opération consiste à le chauffer a 120° à la suite de quoi il perd
¾ de son eau. La poudre obtenue, mise au contact de l'eau,
absorbe de nouveau ce qu'elle a perdu et avant de se solidifier,
forme une masse plastique utilisée dans toutes les opérations de
moulage. Chauffe a 200°, le gypse perd toute son eau ainsi que sa
faculté de la réabsorber.
Cette nouvelle forme est appelée anhydrite, variété qui peut se
rencontrer à l'état naturel.

80   tant et si bien que sa floraison légère lui a fait donner le nom
de « brouillard ».
Les inflorescences de tous les gypsophiles sont utilisées
pour alléger les compositions florales auxquelles elles sont
associées. Celle du *gypsophile paniculata* se sèchent sans difficulté
pour participer aux bouquets d'hiver.

#81   on peut aussi se munir d'un gypsomètre
pour mesurer la teneur en gypse des phrases

82 $CaSO_4 2H_2O$ est la formule de la plante herbacée qui a pour nom

83   une configuration osseuse

84   sulfate de calcium

85   *phyle*
à fleurs blanches

86   *gyspe*

87   the white suit woman with :

88   L'emploi le plus connu du gypse est la fabrication de plâtre pour moulages. Appelé " verre de Marie ", dans les pays catholiques méditerranéens, on en accrochait des fragments aux statues de la Vierge comme symbole de pureté.

 # 89   Excusez-moi mais à bien y réfléchir
je préfère *gyspe*
à *gypse* ;
c'est plus joli et davantage conforme
à ma dyslexie

 # 90   Mine
the woman with*

 # 91   Mine
By the Sign in

 # 92   rose harsh rose

 # 93   apétale rose ma

 # 94   L'anhydrite naturelle est donc le sulfate de calcium anhydre,
c'est-à-dire sans eau. Cristallisée dans le système orthorhom-
bique, elle donne trois clivages à angle droit.

---

* *Il faut aller vers plus d'élagation*

 # 95   dyslexiquement

 # 96   encore

 # 97   *girargue*

 # 98   et ne change rien à la définition

 # 99   puisque je suis la femelle du Pygargue

 # 100   *Gigargue, va !*

 # 101   ouais et « je me sens comme un oiseau de nuit qui refuse de se percher même après trois vols alentour »*, d'ailleurs !

 # 102   d'ailleurs, La chouette chuinte ; elle est adepte des chuintantes d'ailleurs, mon texte chuinte ; ille est adepte des chuintantes

---

* *Li* Ts'ing-tchao, *Les Fleurs du cannelier, trad. du chinois par Zheng Su, Orphée, 1990*

 # 103   je balbuzarde tu balbuzardes ille balbuzarde nous balbuzardons

 # 104   Mine by
           the right
           of

 # 105   ta rhodophrase   *by the right*
           elle laisse des ecchymoses   *of the White Election !*

 # 106   et non le choix

 # 107   car sans tige

 # 108   : un minimum dénudé*

---

* *Il faut aller vers plus d'élagation*

 # 109   - Oh arrête de te sacrifier !

- Mais non, je suis désolée, je ne m'atrophie pas !

 # 110   **Chut !** C'est moi qui souffle !

 # 111   Nyctalope !

 # 112   Oui !

 # 113   Nyctalope !

 # 114   Oui !

 # 115   Mince, j'ai mes tulipes !

 # 116   J'aime pas, quand t'as tes tulipes !

 # 117   Chut, c'est moi qui souffle !

 # 118   Nyctalope !

 # 119   Oui !

 # 120   Nyctalope !

 # 121   Oui !

 # 122   La souffleuse c'est moi

 # 123   La souffleuse

 # 124   Si j'écris le rhododendron est un arbre à roses.

Le laurier-rose est un arbre à rose.

Le romarin est une variété de rosée. (marine).

La rosée marine est une variété de gypsophile.

 # 125   En fait, vous aurez compris, que ce projet a plus à voir avec le rhodoïd

 # 126   En sorte que je suis fondée à dire :

 # 127   Il n'est d'action-gypsophile

SANS action rhodoante*

 # 128   Il n'est de gypse qu'avec rose

Il n'est que de rhodophrasé

 # 129   dans la floridée

 # 130   La floridée est une variété de rose marine.

Un sujet épineux, autrement dit !

Et calcaire, tellement !

˙ (rhodoante = roséifiante) : c'est cela le rhodiage:

| # 131 | mi-algue | mi-rhodo |
| | mi-rose | mi-phycée |

 # 132 à base d'acétate de rhodia**
a celluloïd experiment

 # 133 transparente et combustible   hybride

** *Il faut aller vers plus d'élagation*

 # 134 je travaille, tu travailles, nous travaillons dans l'industrie
de la rose,

        ô mon rosiériste !

 # 135 ouvrières parmi les ouvrières
dans la ruche-roseraie

 # 136 Nous fabriquons des mécanismes-pétales
des cépales-horlogeries

 # 137 et nous ne possédons rien

 # 138 si ce n'est que les mots nous possèdent, eux

 # 139 Oh my rosegrower ! IOU
as a rosebay in a rosebed
rose rose rose from the dead
this rosebud-lay
rose to the bait
just for you

140   Pour éviter le pourrissement – quelle drôle d'idée ! –,
ôter les feuilles basses de la tige.*

141   : c'est cela le bouturage :

142   Éliminer les feuilles à partir de la base sur les 2/3 de la tige.

143   Limiter la longueur de la bouture entre 7 et 15 cm selon
les espèces, en coupant sous une feuille.

144   Prélever toujours une pousse d'extrémité, si possible
qui n'a pas fleuri.

145   : c'est cela le bouturage :

146   s'enraciner et devenir un végétal autonome.

147   Évidemment, on peut aussi marcotter

148   Mais ça, c'est une affaire, beaucoup plus intime**

---

* *Il faut aller vers plus d'élagation*

** *intimidante, incalculable*

149   une affaire de marcottage

150   consiste à faire émettre des racines à un rameau sans le détacher

de la plante mère.

Il reste ainsi nourri par celle-ci tant qu'il n'est pas capable de

s'alimenter seul.

C'est seulement à ce moment qu'il est " sevré ", c'est-à-dire

détaché.

151   : c'est cela le marcottage :

152   un procédé qui ressemble fort au bouturage mais offre

beaucoup moins de risques.

 # 153 Évidemment, il est différentes sortes de marcottage

-le marcottage en cépée (particulièrement recommandé pour beaucoup d'arbustes d'ornement et pour les portes-greffes fruitiers)*

-le marcottage aérien (souvent conseillé pour les ficus, les **philolendrons**, aralias, etc, dont la base s'est dégarnie de feuilles, mais également applicable à tous les arbres et arbustes d'ornement, conifères etc.)**

 # 154 Mais, personnellement je préfère
le marcottage par couchage

 # 155 Applicable à toutes les espèces
à branches assez souples pour être ployées,
le marcottage par couchage consiste à

---

* Cognassiers, pommiers, pruniers... Rabattre la plante mère : *i.e.* **couper (to cut)** à 10/15 cm de la terre (en hiver) : alors apparaître de nouveaux rameaux à partir des yeux latents. En mai, dès qu'avoir une dizaine de cm de long, butter la touffe avec la terre ou mieux, avec un mélange de sable et de tourbe par moitié.

** Après avoir, au besoin, supprimé les feuilles gênantes, entourer **la tige (the stalk)** d'un film de polyéthylène, maintenu en haut et en bas par une ligature et le remplir d'un mélange assez humide de tourbe et de sable par moitiés.

 # 156 Enterrer une ramification basse dans une petite tranchée creusée
à proximité du pied et maintenue en place par un crochet fiché
dans le sol dur.

 # 157 Révéler verticalement son extrémité et la fixer à un tuteur.
Supprimer les feuilles de la partie enterrée. Reboucher
la tranchée avec un mélange de sable et de tourbe par moitiés.

: C'est cela le marcottage par couchage :

Entaille*

↙

---

0   C'est pacemaker qui ne se dit pas

Ultimes Rognages

Plusieurs stimulateurs cardiaques ont bien voulu régler ma marche, lors de la randonnée, à savoir :

1   Le gypsophile

2   La lecture du Guide Clause *(Traité pratique du jardinage,* Serge Vadé, édité par L. Clause, 21e édition, 1976) auquel les précisions **# 80, # 148 - # 158** doivent beaucoup, complétée par celle de *Minéraux et roches* (Karen Callisen, adaptation française par Jean Orcel et André Ph. Sandrea, Fernand Nathan, collection " Nouveaux Guides du Naturaliste ", 1976) cf. précisions **# 39, # 79, # 88, # 95,** et celle enfin d'un article trouvé dans un Télé 7 jours daté d'avril 2000 *(Multipliez vos plantes,* par Patrick Mioulane), dont s'inspirent largement les précisions **# 22,** et **# 23** doivent leur existence au *Dictionnaire étymologique du Français* (Jacqueline Picoche, *Les usuels du Robert,* 1986) ; les précisions **# 25 - # 32 et # 37,** quant à elles, sont redevables du *Petit Robert* (édition 1988).

3   ROSIER très distinctement tagué en rose fluo

        sur vert sapin (troncs conifères x 2)

        sur la route de *Gros de ça* et de *Pompons* (Morvan)

4   Le bouquet de lilas (parme et + effluves correspondantes

        grenat)

        qui, dans le bus 61, entre Austerlitz et Ledru-Rollin (direction

        Porte des lilas),*

5   **L'auteur tenait à les remercier.**

---

* Quid sit lilac lumen? D'où vient la lumière()lilas? Est-ce dans le pourrissement ou la couleur? (une odeur proche du). On répondra, par la présente, que le lilas n'est en rien liliacée. tout juste oléacée.

Pour éviter le pourrissement
ôter les feuilles basses
de la tige.